Zone Diet

The Ultimate Beginners Guide to the Zone Diet (includes 75 recipes and a 2 week meal plan)

TJ Williams

CONTENTS

CHAPTER 1 – WHAT IS THE ZONE DIET?

As you spend your first few days at your Cross Training gym, you may be very excited to find out more about the various exercises that are involved, weekly training plans, clothing and equipment. A well balanced diet plan can be overlooked at times, but it's a crucial component to providing you with the fuel to get the fitness, performance and the physique of your dreams.

I've worked with hundreds of clients over the last couple of years who misinterpret the meaning of training hard as many of them used to think that bodybuilding or fitness is done only at the gym. But that is not true. There is a popular saying across the fitness industry that states 30% of the fitness you gain is from the gym and 70% from the kitchen. The exact percentage is likely to fluctuate based on the individual and their goals for training, but the premise is accurate. Most of your gains (approx. 2/3 to 3/4) will be made from nutrition alone. Yes, you heard it right! So, without further ado let me introduce you to the two main diet forms, tried and tested by athletes all over the world, that will help you build up strength, fitness and confidence to take on the challenges of Cross Training head on!

While your personal trainer may have talked to you about 'Paleo Diet', which is a very popular nutrition strategy, they may have omitted another useful dietary routine going by the name of the 'Zone Diet'. What is the Zone Diet? This is a diet form that primarily consists of consuming foods with high protein and low carbohydrates on 5 equally balanced meals that span throughout the day.

Origins of Zone Diet

Barry Sears is the developer of the Zone Diet who started working on this plan in 1970, when his father suffered a premature death at the age of 53, due to a heart attack. Over the years, he studied the effects of fats and other nutrients on the human heart that may lead to cardiovascular diseases. He consequently attained a Ph. D. in biochemistry, and went on to be revered as one of the best contributors in the world of food and nutrition. He published his first book Enter the Zone in 1995, which went on to become a bestseller as countless people were reaping the benefits of his tireless research. Today, Barry Sears enjoys the status of being a multi-millionaire and author of dozen other books about cooking, nutrition and balanced diets. He even has a website of his own that gains attention of thousands of people across the world.

Basics of Zone Diet and how it works

Now that you are all excited after reading about the founder of Zone Diet and its illustrious origin, allow me to walk you through few basics that will help you get started right away.

- This dietary form works with the main intention of optimizing your body's metabolism and help shed the extra fat through regulation of blood sugar.

- It is also known as the 40:30:30 diet plan, implies the ratio of carbohydrates, proteins and fat intake.

- Optimum carbohydrate intake can be measured by curling hands into two fists.

- Protein amount that each meal should consist of can be measured in relation to the thickness and size of your palm. Equal amounts of protein to that of the palm is considered optimum.

- Fats should be consumed in accordance with the size of your tip of the thumb.

- Zone Diet is accomplished by eating 3 meals and 2 snacks every day with breakfast being taken ideally within one hour after waking up.

- The lunch should be preceded by a snack that has to be consumed two hours prior and at least 4 hours after having breakfast.

- A nutritious snack should follow lunch after 4-5 hours and the ideal time for dinner is set at least 2 hours later of the previous snack.

- Remember to drink lots of water to keep your body hydrated throughout the day and flush out toxins that may cause harm to your metabolic rate.

You may need to follow up this diet strategy with supplements consisting of various vitamins and minerals to keep the body in top-shape. To attain an optimal body fat percentage you must resist every urge to binge on unhealthy foods that not only take you out of the diet plan but may also cause un-repairable damage in the long run. Listen to me closely when I tell you this; there are no shortcuts to success, only hard work and perseverance will get you to your goal.

Benefits of Zone Diet

The benefits of Zone Dieting are exemplary, and are sure to fetch results if followed up without fail. Some of the benefits you reap by conforming to this diet plan are:

1. Permanent weight loss of around 1-1.5 pounds per week

2. Prevention of cardiovascular diseases and overall improvement of physical health

3. Better immune system accompanied by sound metal health

4. Decrease in the signs of aging because of improved skin tone and overall physique

While the aforementioned benefits were intended to be for the general public, a Cross Training athlete should get more from the Zone Diet plan. I will discuss this later in the book.

What advantages does Zone Diet have over Paleo diet?

The paleo diet is also known as 'Paleolithic diet' or 'Caveman diet', as it involves consuming foods that drove out Paleolithic ancestors. The primary food that this diet consists of are meat, organic nuts, berries and other kinds of fruit that are found in abundance in nature. While the thought of following a Paleolithic regime may sound tempting to most people since it is easier to maintain, the Zone Diet has many advantages over this one that you cannot overlook.

- While the Paleo diet heavily relies on heavy intake of protein, the Zone Diet looks to optimize nutrition intake by introducing a healthy mix of carbohydrates and fat as well.

- Even though countless number of professional Cross Training coaches prefer the Paleo diet, they are slightly outnumbered by Zone followers to believe in overall development of the mind and body.

- In today's time and age, foraging for nuts and berries are near to impossible so chances are that you will visit the local supermarket to gather your "hunt". But guess what? Not every dried fruit and nut you buy is organic. This is where Zone Diet takes the leading edge.

- Most people do not realize how their dietary routine impacts their life, so they try 'in trend' plans they read in newspapers and magazines. This is the wrong approach in my opinion. Thorough research that was conducted via scientific experiments and surveys revealed that people who follow Zone Diet are more happy with their health and conscious of general outlook of life. This is our overall goal. Many diets deprive the body of the nutrition it needs, and results in a weak and unhappy individual.

- This plan is divided into blocks so there is no need to go through the rigorous process of counting your nutritional intake every time you have a meal. Unlike Paleo diet, the Zone form of dieting has been proven to help lose fat and gain muscle mass quickly by the Scientific American Frontiers.

- The Zone Diet has withstood the test of time and countless scientific scrutiny to emerge victorious as the best plan for not only Cross Training athletes worldwide, but for any human. This is only possible when the specific dietary plan yields results for overwhelming number of people.

CHAPTER 2 – THE ZONE DIET 'DO'S & DON'TS'

Now that you're acquainted with the basics, functions and benefits of Zone dieting over other plans, you are now ready to move on to the next step. In this section, I'm going to tell you about foods that should make their way into your plate and the one that you should avoid whenever you can. Relax, you can still hang out with your friends and go out to eat outside of your diet plan once a week. There is no need to fret as the Zone Diet covers countless types of nutritious foods that you can introduce to your daily intake and not lose the mettle of your taste buds.

What to eat?

There are a huge amount of options to the foods you can eat with the Zone Diet. I've gone a step further in this book to provide you with 75 recipes to help get you started and inspire you. I've also put them into a 2 week meal plan, so you can see how to structure a Zone Diet into your life over a couple of weeks. Here's a brief list of some of the foods that are included in the Zone Diet:

- Eggplant
- Salmon
- Tuna
- Sea Bass
- Almonds
- Beans
- Soy Cheese
- Blueberries
- Beef Tenderloin
- Turkey Breast
- Chicken Breast
- Pork Tenderloin

- Zucchini
- Parsley
- Oats
- Broccoli

What to avoid?

The previous list of foods that are accepted in the Zone Diet, won't be too shocking to most people. Now that you have started working out, some of the foodstuffs that you should cut out from your diet are:

- Dairy products like Ice-cream, Yoghurt, etc. and other kinds of food made from whole milk.

- Red meat is best avoided along with consumption of organs like liver or egg yolk.

- Not all fruits and veggies are the best way to go either as corn, bananas, raisins, carrots, mangoes and other kinds of fruit juices/shakes can work against your metabolic function.

- Avoid white bread, white rice, sweetened cereal and other type of baked goods. Oh! Did I mention to avoid potatoes? Well, there you have it.

- To reach the zenith of your physical capacity, you must avoid every type of addictive substances like cigarettes, alcohol, "diet-drinks" and other substances that contain caffeine.

Your aim should be to strike a perfect balance between consumption of carbohydrates, fats and protein so that you remain active throughout the day with minimal chances of getting fatigue. Cross Training focuses on overall development, so should your diet plan.

Don't be deterred by the list of foods that are not included in the Zone Diet. There are a huge amount of wonderful options for you. As I mentioned earlier, I will provide you with 75 recipes that conform to the Zone Diet. This is far from an extensive list. You can mix and match the recipes I provide and you can research other dishes online to keep your nutrition interesting (if you feel the need to).

I would also encourage you to try the Zone Diet for at least 2 weeks before judging what it 'might' be like. Most of my clients are surprised how easy it is to follow, how tasty the dishes are, and more importantly, how great they feel following it.

CHAPTER 3 – HOW TO APPLY THE ZONE DIET TO YOUR TRAINING PLAN

Now that you are extensively aware of what type of food you should eat, it's time to focus on how to implement your daily meals according to your exercise time and type. In this section, I will discuss with you my knowledge that I have gained over the last decade working as a professional Cross Trainer. Some of the topics that will be discussed here are the 40:30:30 rule, Zone blocking, calculation of optimum zone block per meal and how NOT to fall out of your Zone Diet plan whenever you're eating out.

Essentials of 40:30:30 rule

The 40:30:30 rule makes up for the most essential element of the Zone Diet plan. As discussed earlier, to facilitate fast growth of muscles and loss of fat the human body needs to be subjected to intake of 40% Carbohydrates, 30% protein and 30% fat on a daily basis to stay in prime shape. According to Sears, this balanced diet helps maintain proper hormonal balance or as he likes to call it "to stay in the zone". It has been proven beyond any reasonable doubt that hormones are what drives us to function throughout the day by balancing Insulin, Glucagon and Eicosanoids.

What are the functions of these hormones? Well, Insulin is a storage hormone that helps you store fat, Glucagon is a mobilization hormone that regulates the passage of carbohydrates that are stored in the body and Eacosanoids are the primary hormones, in charge of operation of other types of hormones that are present in our system. As you may have guessed it by now, excess production of any of these three hormones can lead to disastrous effects. This is exactly what Zone Diet helps to regulate.

Zone Blocking and How to Measure It

The Zone Diet is measured in blocks, planning meals according to Zone block charts is your best bet in achieving hormonal balance along with all-round mental and physical wellbeing. Whether you are a pro athlete looking to shift to Zone based diet or a person who is just starting out with Cross Training, this form of dieting will ensure that you get all the required nutrients to keep you at the top of your game all day, every day.

To calculate the block requirement, you need to take into account the size and type of your body. Whether male or female, big or large or somewhere in between, I've got just the right kinds of Zone blocks ready for you. Working as a fitness expert and nutritionist, I can safely assume that the initial phases of figuring out the ideal diet plan may seem to be confusing. But, hang in there! I'm here to simplify everything you need to know about Zone blocking.

CHAPTER 4 – ZONE FOODS

Zone Food Blocks

Each meal in the Zone diet consists of protein, carbohydrate and fat blocks. A different amount of PRO, CAR, and FAT is required to meet a single block. Here's the individual breakdown of each macronutrient:

Protein Block – A single protein block has 7g of protein. A man requires four protein blocks (28g) and a woman requires only three protein blocks per meal (21g).

Carbohydrate Block – A single carbohydrate block has 9g of carbohydrates. An average woman requires three carbohydrate blocks in every meal (27g). An average male requires four carbohydrate blocks (36g).

Fat Block – A single fat block has 3g of fat. An average female requires three fat blocks (9g). An average male requires four fat blocks (12g) per meal.

Key to the Zone Blocks

- The number of blocks you'll require per meal will depend on whether you are male or female.

- Consume the same number of carbohydrate blocks as protein.

- Consume the same number of fat blocks as protein.

Protein Block Examples

Haddock. 1 and ½ ounces of haddock = 1 Protein Block.

Cod. 1 and ½ ounces of cod = 1 Protein Block.

Crabmeat. 1 and ½ ounces of crabmeat = 1 Zone Block.

Egg Whites (or Egg Substitute). 2 egg whites or ¼ cup of egg substitute = 1 Protein Block.

Milk (Skim). 8 ounces of skim milk = 1 Protein Block.

Salmon. 1 and ½ ounces of salmon = 1 Protein Block.

Sea Bass. 1 and ½ ounces of sea bass = 1 Protein Block.

Tuna. 1 ounce of tuna steak or 1 and ½ ounces of canned tuna = 1 Protein Block.

Cottage Cheese (Low Fat). ¼th cup of low-fat cottage cheese = 1 Protein Block.

Soy Milk. 8 ounces of soy milk = 1 Protein Block.

Beef Tenderloin, Well-Trimmed. 1 ounce of well-trimmed beef tenderloin = 1 Protein Block.

Carbohydrate Block Examples

Cauliflower. 4 cups of cauliflower = 1 Carbohydrate Block

Blackberries. 3/4 cup of blackberries = 1 Carbohydrate Block

Blueberries. ½ cup of blueberries = 1 Carbohydrate Block

Broccoli. 3 cups of cooked broccoli = 1 Carbohydrate Block.

Turnip Greens. 4 cups of cooked turnip greens = 1 Carbohydrate Block.

Artichokes. 4 artichokes or 1 cup of artichoke hearts = 1 Carbohydrate Block.

Red Bell Peppers. 2 red peppers = 1 Carbohydrate Block.

Black Beans. ¼ cup of black beans = 1 Carbohydrate Block.

Cabbage. 3 cups of cooked cabbage = 1 Carbohydrate Block.

Eggplant. 1 and ½ cups of cooked eggplant = 1 Carbohydrate Block.

Green Beans. 1 and ½ cups of cooked green beans = 1 Carbohydrate Block.

Lentils. ¼ cup of cooked lentils = 1 Carbohydrate Block.

Oats. 1/3 cup of cooked oatmeal = 1 Carbohydrate Block.

Zucchini. 2 cups of cooked zucchini = 1 Carbohydrate Block.

Fat Block Examples

Almonds. 3 almonds = 1 Fat Block.

Macadamia Nuts. 1 macadamia nut = 1 Fat Block.

Avocados. 1 tablespoon = 1 Zone Block.

Olive Oil. 2/3 teaspoon of olive oil = 1 Fat Block.

Cashews. 3 cashews = 1 Fat Block.

Canola Oil. 2/3 teaspoon of canola oil = 1 Fat Block.

Peanuts. 6 peanuts = 1 Fat Block.

CHAPTER 5 – ZONE RECIPES

As mentioned earlier; attaining the peak of physical fitness involves 30% of workouts and 70% of time spent in the kitchen. Since, you're ready to spend some time prepping up dishes for yourself and family, here's 15 breakfast, lunch, snacks, dinner and dessert recipes that will make anyone a fan of the Zone Diet.

This is not an extensive list of Zone Diet Recipes. You can research alternatives online if you wish to do so. The aim of this chapter is to provide over 2 week's worth of breakfast, lunch, dinner, snack and dessert options for you. You can add or change the recipes with alternative Zone Diet foods to suit your needs. If you're stuck on what to cook, these recipes will be the perfect starting place for you, and I'd still encourage you to expand your culinary skills and use this list as inspiration to create your own dishes.

Breakfast Recipes

Breakfast Sandwich

Ingredients:

- 1 or 2 brown breads
- 1 scrambled egg (no yolk)
- 1 oz. of cheese
- Serve with macadamia nuts
- Slice of ham (optional)

Preparation:

- Scramble an egg in advance.
- Put the eggs, cheese and slice of ham between bread.

Fruit Salad

Ingredients:

- ½ cup cottage cheese
- ¼ cantaloupe
- ½ cup grapes
- ½ cup strawberries

Preparation:

- Take all your ingredients and mix them together in a large bowl.

Apple Cinnamon Crepe

Ingredients:

- ½ cup egg whites
- 1 tbsp. olive oil
- 1/3 cup soy flour
- 1 cup of skimmed milk
- 1 small finely chopped red apple
- 1/3 cup applesauce unsweetened
- ½ cup cooked oatmeal
- 2 slices of bacon
- ¼ tbsp. of cinnamon powder

Preparation:

- Take a bowl and mix egg whites, oil, flour and milk to a batter. Put a generous amount of olive oil and spray it over either a sauté' pan or a crepe pan.

- Take a quarter of the batter to pan and cover it with another crepe or sauté pan. Cook in medium to high flame so that the crepe does not stick. Turn the crepe over by placing the second pan over the first, and flip it over gracefully. Cook the second side of the crepe for a minute or so.

- Place the oatmeal, applesauce, chopped apples, Canadian bacon and cinnamon to make the filling and cook it in low flame until the apple becomes soft. Serve quickly.

Breakfast Quesadilla

Ingredients:

- 1 corn tortilla
- 1/3 cup chopped onions
- ½ cup black beans
- 1 chopped green pepper (optional)
- 2 eggs fried or scrambled
- 2 oz. cheese
- 4 tbsp. avocado

Preparation:

- Take a small bowl and whisk the eggs, then making a coating of a big skillet with cooking spray. Add eggs and cook it in medium flame until it is completely set.

- Place the corn tortillas on a griddle. Smear the eggs over half of a tortilla and sprinkle the preparation with cheese, avocado, black beans, chopped onion and green pepper.

Nut & Berry Smoothie

Ingredients:

- 2 cups of milk
- 2 tbsp. of protein powder

- ½ frozen blueberries
- 1 cup of strawberries
- cashew nuts, handful

Preparation:

- Put it in a blender and let it rip!!
- Sprinkle a healthy amount of cashew nuts over the drink

Steak and Eggs

Ingredients:

- 3 oz. grilled steak
- 1 egg,
- 1 slice of buttered toast
- ½ of a cantaloupe

Preparation:

- Put the steak on a grill and heat in medium flame till the stake acquires a brownish color.
- Make the egg separately and get the bread ready by smearing it with butter. Use cantaloupe to garnish.
- Put all of these on a plate and eat to your heart's content.

Oatie Porridge

Ingredients:

- 1 cup of oats
- ½ cup grapes
- 3/4 cup cottage cheese
- 2 tbsp. of walnuts
- 1 tsp. cinnamon powder

Preparation:

- First cook the oatmeal in a regular fashion. Make sure that the final product is a bit watery.
- Mix grapes, cottage cheese and walnuts to the oatmeal.
- Add cinnamon powder to add some spice!

Rice Bowl

Ingredients:

- 1/3 cup Zone orzo
- 2/3 cup semi-skimmed milk
- 1 tsp. vanilla extract
- 1 tbsp. Polaner sugar free preserve
- ¼ tbsp. pumpkin spice
- 1 ½ tbsp. almonds
- ¼ cup strawberries

Preparation:

- In a bowl, combine milk, fruits, pumpkin pie spice, Zone orzo and simmer slowly for 10-12 minutes.
- When the mixture has thickened, sprinkle pumpkin pie spice or a small amount of cinnamon.
- Stir again; when done, you serve it hot or cold.

Blueberry Ricotta Oatmeal

Ingredients:

- 2 scoops of zone protein powder (14 g)
- 3/4 cup cooked oats
- ½ cup blueberries

- ¼ cup low-fat ricotta cheese
- 2 tbsp. of powdered almonds

Preparation:

- First, cook the oatmeal. When done, all and stir the protein power to form a mix.
- Put the mixture in a serving bowl and mix with the blueberries. Microwave for 2 minutes.
- Gently spread the almonds and low-fat ricotta to act as garnishing.

Breakfast Tart

Ingredients:

- ½ cup finely chopped onions
- 18 chopped olives
- 1 cup mozzarella cheese
- 4 oz. semi-skimmed milk
- 1 ½ cup of egg whites
- 1 ½ tbsp. olive oil
- 1 tbsp. dried basil
- 1 tbsp. dried dill
- Pinch of seasoning
- 1 tbsp. lemon, squeezed
- 1 tbsp. ginger root
- 2 kiwis
- 1 pear
- 1 cup of frozen cherries

Preparation:

- Pre-heated the oven to 350F.

- Grease your baking tray.

- Add all the half diced onions, half diced pepper mozzarella cheese and the olives.

- Take rest of the onion, tomatoes, olive oil, eggs, salt and pepper, spices and put it inside of a blender to mix it evenly until smooth.

- Pour this mixture in to a pan and keep it on bake for 25-30 minutes. Notice that the mixture has attained a puffy form and is golden brown in colour.

- Make the fruit salad by mixing the cut fruit into a bowl and spray enough amounts of lemon juice. Serve while it's hot!

Banana, Almond and Coconut Smoothie

Ingredients:

- 2 cups unsweetened coconut milk

- ½ cup frozen or fresh banana slices

- 3 tbsp. almond butter

- 1 tsp. vanilla

- 3 tbsp. almond butter

- 2 cups unsweetened coconut milk

Preparation:

- Blend all ingredients in a blender and serve.

Blueberry Breakfast Cookies

Ingredients:

- 3 cups almond flour

- 1 tsp baking soda

- ½ tsp cinnamon
- 1 tsp salt
- 2 chia eggs
- 1 tsp vanilla extract
- ¼ cup almond milk
- 1 cup blueberries
- ½ cup almond butter

Preparation:

- Preheat oven to 375°F/ 190°C.
- In a bowl, combine the baking soda, almond flour, cinnamon and salt.
- Then add the wet ingredients; vanilla extract, chia eggs, almond butter, almond milk.
- Mix to combine.
- Now, add the blueberries, stir carefully to combine and let it sit for 2-3 minutes.
- Scoop 1 tbsp. of the dough onto a sheet of parchment paper and slightly flatten the top of the dough.
- Bake in the oven for 15 minutes or until light brown and check if they're cooked through with a knife.
- Take the tray out of the oven and leave to cool on the kitchen top or stove.

Zucchini Fritters

Ingredients:

- 2 medium zucchini (grated)
- 1 chia egg (beaten)
- ¼ cup coconut flour

- 1 tsp black pepper
- 2 tsp sea salt
- ¼ tsp cayenne pepper
- Coconut oil for cooking

Preparation:

- Shred the zucchini in a box grater, then put the shredded zucchini into a large bowl. Sprinkle with sea salt and toss well for even coverage. Leave for 10 mins.
- Now, scoop up a handful of the shredded zucchini and squeeze out the excess water and place into a difference bowl. Add the chia egg, pepper and coconut flour. Stir to combine.
- Heat a large skillet over a medium to low heat and melt a large spoonful of coconut oil into the pan. In a ¼ cup of zucchini, add the zucchini into the pan by turning over the cup into the pan to make a round patty and flatten the patty. You should be able to fit around 4 to 5 fritters onto one pan at a time.
- Cook each side for 3-5 minutes until a nice brown color and repeat with the next batch, remember to re-add the coconut oil with every new batch.
- Once cooked, place them onto a metal rack to drain any excess oil and for them to cool off.

Carrot Muffins

Ingredients:

- ¼ coconut flour
- 1 tsp ground cinnamon
- ¼ sea salt
- 3 large chia eggs
- ¼ tsp baking soda

- 1 cup grated carrots
- ¼ cup grapeseed oil
- 1 tbsp. vanilla extract
- ¼ cup currants
- ¼ cup yacon syrup

Preparation:

- In a medium sized mixing bowl combine the dry ingredients; coconut flour, cinnamon, salt and baking soda.
- In a large mixing bowl, add and mix the wet ingredients; vanilla extract, chia eggs, yacon syrup and grapeseed oil.
- Now, add the wet ingredients into the dry ingredient bowl and blend it with the grated carrots and currants.
- Grease a muffin tin with grapeseed oil, spoon approx. 1 tbsp. of batter into each muffin tin cup.
- Bake for 10 minutes or until golden brown at 350°F.
- Set aside to cool and then serve.

Apricot Power Bars

Ingredients:

- 1 cup dried apricots
- 2 chia eggs
- 2 cups pecans
- 1 tbsp. vanilla extract
- ¼ tsp sea salt
- ½ cup chocolate chips (optional)

Preparation:

- Put pecans and apricots into a food processor and blend until a gravel texture.
- Add in the chia eggs, vanilla extract and sea salt and blend until the texture is coarse.
- Now, empty the mixture into a bowl and fold in the chocolate chips (again, optional.).
- Spread the mixture onto a baking dish evenly.
- Bake at 350°F for 25 mins.
- Cool, cut and serve.

Lunch Recipes

Vegetable Stuffed Cabbage

<u>Ingredients</u>:

- ½ cabbage
- 2 ½ cups chestnuts (sliced)
- 1 cup carrots
- 1 cup parsnips
- ½ onion
- ½ cup white wine
- 1 tsp extra virgin olive oil
- Salt and pepper

<u>Preparation</u>:

- Peel the carrots and parsnips with a vegetable peeler, then dice with a knife.
- Peel the onion and finely chop. Cook the onions in a pan with the olive oil until they soften slightly and add the chestnuts and cook for an additional 2 minutes.
- Then add the chopped carrot and parsnip, lower the heat and cook for another 2 – 3 minutes.
- Deglaze with white wine, season with salt and pepper in the pan.
- Now, pick the leaves off of the cabbage and set aside.
- In a robot, mix the carrot, parsnip, chestnuts and the remaining cabbage. Make small balls with the mixture, take a leaf and place the ball in the middle of it. Now fold the leaves over.
- Repeat with every leaf.
- Serve on a plate with salad.

Udon Noodle Salad with Almond Dressing

Ingredients:

- 1 packet of organic udon noodles
- ½ cup sliced spring onions
- 3 shredded/grated carrots
- 2 cups shredded cabbage
- 1 sliced red onion
- 1 clove garlic
- 1 cup baby spinach
- 1 cup coriander

Sauce:

- 2 tsp sunflower seeds
- 1 tsp chili powder
- 1 tsp tamari powder
- 2 tbsp. premium soy sauce
- 1 tsp almond oil
- 1 juiced lime
- 1 lemongrass stalk (white part)
- ½ cup warm water

Preparation:

- Bring a pot of water to boil over a medium heat.
- Add in the noodles to the water and cook for 8 – 10 mins. Then, drain and rinse under cold water in a colander. Set aside.
- Blend all of the ingredients for the sauce together until smooth. Set aside.
- Put all of the vegetables into a bowl and toss in the noodles. Then, add the sauce and gently toss to combine.

- Top with the spring onions, sunflower seeds and coriander.
- Serve hot or cold.

Cabbage, Lettuce and Leek Stir fry

Ingredients:

- 1 cup leek
- 3 cups cabbage
- ½ box of noodles
- 1 cup lettuce
- 3 tbsp. premium grade soy sauce
- ¼ cup organic tofu

Preparation:

- In a medium to low heat place the wok over the heat and add the coconut oil into the pan.
- Add the leak, cabbage and lettuce into the pan and fry for 2-5 minutes.
- Boil the noodles and drain. Add it to the wok and add the soy sauce. Fry for another 2 minutes and transfer to a bowl.
- Cube ¼ cup of tofu and add to the stir fry.
- Serve.

Jamaican Rice & Peas

Ingredients:

- 1 ½ cups brown rice
- 1 large can of kidney beans
- 1 onion
- 4 garlic cloves

- 1 tbsp. fresh grated ginger
- 2 tbsp. dried thyme
- 2 bay leaves
- 2 cups coconut milk
- 1 tbsp. of coconut oil
- 1 cup vegetable broth
- Dash of lime juice
- 1 tsp of salt

Preparation:

- Peel and chop the onion, place in a preheated medium pan and sauté until lightly brown, add the chopped garlic, rice and oil. Cook for a few minutes then add the garlic and water.
- Drain and rinse the kidney beans, then add them and to the pan with the thyme and bay leaves. Allow to simmer for a few minutes.
- Cook on a low heat for thirty to forty minutes, until all the excess liquid has evaporated.
- Remove from the heat and set aside for ten minutes.
- Taste and season appropriately, remove the bay leaves and finish off with a splash of lime juice.

Lentil Dahl

Ingredients:

- 1 potato
- ½ onion
- 1 tomato
- 3 cups frozen vegetables
- 1 cup chickpeas

- 1 tsp mustard
- ½ tsp turmeric
- 4 ½ cups water
- Salt

Preparation:

- Peel and chop the ½ onion, sauté in a pan with the mustard at a low to medium heat.
- Then peel and chop the potato into small cubes and when the onion golden add the mixed vegetables, potato turmeric and salt.
- Place the mixture added with water into a pressure cooker and heat until steam in visible.
- Once steam is visible reduce heat and simmer for a further fifteen minutes.
- Once the mixture is cooked, allow to cool down.
- Chop the tomato and drain the chick peas, add to the mixture and taste, season if required.

Mushroom & Tofu Stroganoff

Ingredients:

- 1 cup cremini mushrooms
- 1 cup fusilli pasta
- 1 onion
- 2 ½ tofu
- 4 cloves of garlic
- 2 tbsp. of tomato paste
- 1 tsp of dried thyme
- 3/4 cup cashew nuts (soaked 2hrs)
- 1 ½ cups vegetable broth

- 2 tbsp. of olive oil
- ½ tsp of salt
- ½ cup of dry white wine

Preparation:

- Slice the tofu into even 4 inch strips.
- Cook the pasta for twenty minutes in a pot of boiling water until ready, then drain.
- Place the cashews in a mixer with the vegetable stock and mix until smooth.
- Preheat a large saucepan and sauté the tofu until golden brown, then take off the heat and rest at the side.
- Peel and thinly slice the onion, place along with the oil in the pan vacated by the tofu and sauté for a further five minutes and add the garlic.
- Slice the mushrooms and add them to the saucepan along with the thyme, cook for a further 5 minutes.
- Then add the wine, tomato paste and seasoning, simmer and reduce the wine.
- Add in the mixture from the blender and cook for a further five minutes.
- Gently add the tofu to the sauce and coat generously.
- Finally serve the tofu and on top of the cooked pasta.

Quinoa Pasta, Peas & Kale with a Vegan Alfredo Sauce

Ingredients:

- 4 stalks kale
- 8 oz. quinoa pasta
- ½ cup cashew nuts

- ½ cup peas
- ¼ cup yeast
- ¼ cup onion powder
- 2 cloves garlic
- 1 ½ cups almond milk
- 3 tbsp. of water
- 1 tbsp. of lemon juice
- Pinch of salt and pepper

Preparation:

- Place the pasta in a pot of boiling water for twenty minutes until firm to the bite.
- Into a preheated pan sauté the minced garlic and add the kale, a few minutes later add in the peas and add the water and seasoning.
- Simmer until the water is gone.
- While that is simmering, place three more tablespoons of water, almond milk, yeast, cashews, onion powder, lemon juice and seasoning into a blender and mix until thoroughly smooth.
- Place the resulting sauce in a large pan and heat until thickened.
- Once thickened remove from the heat and add the pasta and the other ingredients to the sauce, taste and season.

Stuffed Bell Peppers

Ingredients:

- 4 bell peppers
- 2 cloves garlic
- 1 cup diced onions
- 1 cup frozen spinach

- 1 cup string beans
- 1 cup cooked brown rice
- 1 cup chopped mushroom
- 1 cup chopped peppers
- 1 ½ cups tomato soup
- 1 cup chopped tomatoes
- 1 cup cooked chopped carrots
- Pinch of pepper
- Chopped parsley for seasoning

Preparation:

- Clean and chop all vegetables, cut tops off of the peppers remove seeds, cook the rice, leave to drain and cool.
- Sauté the chopped vegetables in a pan with water for roughly ten minutes.
- Once cooked mix with the rice and add one cup of tomato sauce to flavour.
- Coat bottom of an oven tray with tomato sauce and place the prepared peppers onto the tray, fill with the vegetable mix.
- Once all the peppers are filled wrap the tray in foil and place in a preheated oven at 400 degrees for forty to forty five minutes until cooked.

Tomato & Aubergine Pasta

Ingredients:

- 1 can of chopped tomatoes
- 1 chopped onion
- 2 cloves garlic
- 2 aubergines

- 5 cups of rigatoni
- 5 tablespoons of olive oil
- Pinch of finely chopped basil

Preparation:

- Place the rigatoni into a pot of boiling water and cook for twenty minutes, then drain when cooked.
- Prepare and cut the aubergines into 2 cm slice, also peel and chop the garlic in to a paste.
- Sauté the chopped onions, garlic and basil stalks in a preheated pan with half the olive oil.
- Once the onions and golden brown add the tomatoes and cook for a further 20 minutes.
- Place the aubergines in another preheated pan and fry until golden.
- Then add the golden aubergines and rigatoni into the tomato sauce and mix well.

Coconut Chana Saag

Ingredients:

- 1 onion
- 1 large can whole tomatoes
- 2 medium cans of chickpeas
- 1 large can coconut milk
- 1 ½ Kale
- 3 cloves garlic
- 2 tbsp. minced ginger
- 2 tbsp. mild curry powder
- ¼ tsp garam masala

- ½ tsp ground cumin
- ¼ tsp cayenne pepper
- 2 tbsp. of extra virgin olive oil
- 1 tsp of salt
- Pinch of ground black pepper

Preparation:

- Dice the onion, add into a preheated pan on a low-medium heat for five minutes, then add the ginger and chopped garlic.
- Now add all the spices (cumin, cayenne pepper, curry powder, garam masala, salt and pepper).
- Rinse and drain the chickpeas, then add them and the tomatoes to the mixture.
- Allow to cook at a low temperature for ten minutes.
- Chop the kale and add, allowing to cook for five minutes.
- Finally, add the coconut milk and season as appropriate.

Curried Potato

Ingredients:

- 4 potatoes
- 1 onion
- 1 piece fresh ginger
- 1 large can of diced tomatoes
- 1 large can of chickpeas
- 1 large can of peas
- 1 large can of coconut milk
- 3 cloves garlic
- 4 tsp garam masala
- 4 tsp mild curry powder

- 2 tsp ground cumin
- 1 ½ tsp cayenne pepper
- 2 tbsp. coconut oil
- 2 tsp of salt

Preparation:

- Peel and dice the potatoes, place in a pot and cover with water, add salt and lightly boil for fifteen to twenty minutes until soft, then drain.
- Place a large skillet on the stove and heat with a coating of the coconut oil.
- Peel and dice the onion, garlic and ginger, add the onion and garlic to the skillet and sauté for around five minutes.
- Now add the spices to the onion (cayenne pepper, cumin, garam masala, ginger, mild curry powder and salt), cook for a further few minutes.
- Open and drain the chickpeas, tomatoes and peas and add them along with the potatoes to the skillet.
- Then add the coconut milk and allow to infuse for ten minutes.

Tortilla Wraps Tex-Mex Style

Ingredients:

- 3 chopped scallions
- 1 can of black beans
- 4 gluten-free flour tortillas
- ¼ cup of chopped bell pepper
- 2 cloves of garlic
- 2 tbsp. of orange juice
- 2 tbsp. of lime juice

- Salsa
- Pinch of salt and cayenne pepper

Preparation:

- Peel and roughly chop the scallions and garlic.
- Open the can of black beans, drain and rinse.
- In your blender add the garlic, cayenne pepper, salt, lime juice and orange juice. Process the mixture until very smooth.
- Remove from the blender and place in a large mixing bowl, add the chopped scallions and bell peppers to the mixture.
- Place the mixture evenly in the centre of the tortillas and fold tightly and fish off with a topping of the salsa.

Layered Vegetable Bake

Ingredients:

- ¼ cup almond butter
- 2 crushed garlic cloves
- 1 medium leek (white part, thinly sliced.)
- 2 cups baby spinach
- 4 cups vegetable squash (thinly sliced)
- 2 cups potatoes (thinly sliced)
- ½ cup grated cheese
- ½ cup cream cheese
- 3 chia eggs
- 1/3 cup cream
- 1 tbsp. thyme leaves
- Salt and pepper

Preparation:

- Heat coconut in a frying pan over a medium heat and sauté the leek and garlic for 5 minutes.
- Then add the spinach and cook for a further minute.
- In a glass oven dish, layer half of the potatoes in the base. Then, top with the spinach and leek mixture. To finish, top with the remaining potatoes and sprinkle with grated cheese over the top.
- In a mixing bowl, whisk together the chia eggs, cream cheese, thyme, cream and salt and pepper.
- Pour the cream cheese mixture over the dish and bake at 200°C for 40 -45 minutes.
- Plate accordingly and serve with your favourite salad.

Curry Tomato Soup with Zucchini Noodles

Ingredients:

- 1 medium zucchini (grated)
- 3 cups tomatoes (diced)
- 1 large yellow onion
- ¼ cup fresh basil
- ½ tsp red pepper flakes
- ¼ tsp cumin
- 1 can coconut milk
- 1 tbsp. coconut oil
- 2 cups water/vegetable broth
- 1 tbsp. red curry paste

Preparation:

- In a large pot, over a medium heat, add the coconut oil. Then, add the onions and let it sauté for 5 minutes or until softened.

- Now, add in the tomatoes, red pepper flakes, curry paste, water, basil and salt. Turn the heat up a little and bring to a boil, reduce the heat and cover with a lid. Let it simmer for 15 minutes.
- Then add the coconut milk after 10 minutes and stir, let it simmer for another 5 minutes.
- Once cooked, remove from heat and let it rest on top of the stove to cool for a few minutes.
- Puree the soup with an immersion blender.
- Serve in a separate bowl and add basil and the shredded zucchini (raw) on top.

Vegan California Sushi Roll

Ingredients:

- ¼ cup roasted red pepper
- ½ cup prepared sushi rice
- ¼ cup tofu
- 2 tsp vegan mayonnaise
- 1 sheet of nori (dried seaweed)
- ¼ cucumber (sliced)
- ½ avocado (sliced)

Preparation:

- In a blender or food processor, add mayo, red pepper and tofu and blend until smooth.
- Lay a sheet of nori on a bamboo sushi mat, spread the rice over the nori, leaving one or two inches on one side uncovered.
- Then, spread the red pepper mixture around the center of the sheet and top with the avocado and cucumber.

- Roll the sushi and cut into 8 pieces. Start by cutting the roll in the middle, then place the two halves against each other then slice through the middle again and cut accordingly.

Dinner Recipes

Gluten Free Cauliflower Salad

Ingredients:

- 1 head cauliflower
- 1 yellow onion
- 2 stalks celery
- 3 hard boiled chia eggs
- 2 tbsp. grapeseed oil
- 1 tbsp. Dijon/French mustard
- Pinch of sea salt

Preparation:

- Chop the cauliflower into small florets.
- Steam the cauliflower on a stove on top of a saucepan until tender.
- Allow to cool and then transfer to a large bowl.
- Dice the chia eggs, celery and onion and add it to the cauliflower bowl.
- Make the sauce by adding the grapeseed oil, French mustard and sea salt in a bowl and whisking with a fork. Then add it to the cauliflower.

Roasted Butternut Squash with Broccoli Pesto Filling

Ingredients:

- 1 organic butternut squash
- 4 florets of broccoli
- 10 whole Brazilian nuts
- 1 tbsp. capers

- 1/3 cup pomegranate seeds
- 1 tsp ground pepper
- 2 tbsp. basil
- ½ cup extra virgin olive oil
- 1 ½ tsp sea salt

Preparation:

- Preheat the oven to 338°F.
- On a sheet lined baking tray, place the 2 halves of the butternut squash onto it with the seeds scooped out.
- Drizzle with the olive oil and sea salt and pepper.
- Place in the oven for approx.45 minutes, until the squash is soft.
- To make the broccoli pesto; in a food processor place the olive oil, brazil nuts, broccoli, basil and a pinch of sea salt and blend, add more olive oil if it is not smooth enough.
- Now, add the pesto mix onto the butternut squash. Add capers and drizzle olive oil on top. Serve.

Roasted Red Pepper & Pesto Courgette with Savory Scones

Ingredients:

- 1 red pepper (chopped and roasted)
- 4 medium courgettes
- ¼ cup pine nuts
- 1 garlic clove
- ¼ cup basil
- ¼ cup rocket
- ½ cup extra virgin olive oil

For the savory scone:

- 4 cups gluten-free self-raising flour
- 4 tbsp. golden caster sugar
- 1 cup almond butter
- 1 tsp baking powder
- ¼ tsp salt
- 1 ½ cup natural yogurt
- 4 tbsp. almond milk
- 1 tsp vanilla extract
- 2 chia eggs

Preparation:

- For the courgette; using a spiralizer create your courgette noodles and place them into a serving bowl.
- For the savory scones; pour salt, flour and baking powder into a food processor, pulse. Then add in the butter and pulse it again, until it's mixed in. Pulse in the sugar and then pour the mixture into a large mixing bowl and make a well in the middle.
- In a saucepan, heat up the milk, vanilla extract and yogurt for around 1 min. Then pour it into the flour mix bowl. Take a wooden spoon and mix the ingredients in the bowl until it turns to dough and then work it with your hands until it turns into a dough ball.
- Take the dough ball and place it onto a surface worktop that's been dusted with flour, knead the dough a couple of times with your palms. Then, take a rolling pin and roll the dough out 1 ½ inch thick. Take a round glass cup and cutout the dough shapes and place them onto a sheet lined baking tray.
- Brush the dough rounds with egg wash and bake for 12 minutes at 220°C, until they have risen and are golden brown. Take out

of the oven, let them cool and then transfer onto a plate and enjoy with the roasted red pepper courgette.

- For the pesto; roast the pepper in the oven at 180°C until roasted and slightly browned.
- In a food processor, place the roasted pepper, pine nuts, basil, rocket, garlic, olive oil and salt and blend. It should be of a medium consistency. Store in a re-sealable jar and place in the fridge.
- Serve the courgette noodles, savoury scones and red pepper pesto together.

Pan-fried Festive Salad

Ingredients:

- 2 cups kale
- 3 cups Brussels sprouts (halved)
- 1 red onion (diced)
- ½ cup cranberries or pomegranate
- ½ cup hazelnuts or almond flakes
- 2 tsp orange zest
- 1 tsp coconut oil
- ½ cup water
- Pinch sea salt

Preparation:

- In a wok, drizzle some coconut oil and add the diced onion and cook over a medium heat until soft.
- Add in the Brussels sprouts and cook for another 3 – 4 minutes. Add ¼ cups of water at a time to give a base for the sprouts to cook on and stopping them from sticking.
- Then, add in the kale and cook for another 2 minutes.

- In a separate pan, toast the hazelnuts and/or almond flakes, then turn off the heat and add it to the sprout pan. Take it off the heat and add the cranberries, orange zest and salt.
- Serve with hash browns.

Ratatouille

Ingredients:

- ½ cup olive oil
- 2 large tomatoes
- 4 cups eggplant
- 1 large onion
- 1 bell pepper (chopped)
- 2 zucchini's
- 4 garlic cloves
- ½ cup chopped parsley
- 10 basil leaves
- Sea salt
- Black pepper

Preparation:

- Place the tomatoes into a pot of boiling water for a minute then place into cold water in a bowl. Once they're cold enough to handle, remove the skin.
- Chop the tomatoes and then put them into a large pot with the ½ cup of olive oil, along with the garlic, parsley and basil.
- Cover the pot partially with water and simmer whilst stirring from time to time, for around 30 minutes or until the tomatoes are well broken down.

- Sprinkle the eggplant with sea salt and put them in a colander and leave in the kitchen sink.

- Place the onions in a frying pan with coconut oil and cook for 10 minutes and season with sea salt.

- Now transfer the onions to a bowl and cook the bell pepper for the same amount of time. Remove and transfer them to the onion bowl.

- Repeat this process for the zucchini, this time only for 6 minutes.

- Pat the eggplants dry and repeat the process, cooking them for about 7 minutes, again adding some olive oil each time.

- Once the tomatoes have simmered on its own for long enough, add the previously cooked vegetables, season generously with sea salt and black pepper, cover with a lid and simmer for about another hour, until all the vegetables are very soft.

- The ratatouille is now ready to serve; it is a staple in many French households.

Spinach Quiche

Ingredients:

- 1 ½ cups fresh chopped spinach
- 5 chia eggs
- ½ cup coconut milk
- ½ medium onion (chopped)
- 1 crushed garlic clove
- ½ tsp baking powder
- Sea salt
- Black pepper

Preparation:

- Preheat oven to 350F.
- In a large mixing bowl, whisk the chia eggs and coconut milk together.
- As you continue to whisk start adding in the onion, garlic, baking powder and spinach.
- Now start greasing your pie dish and pour the mixture in and place in the oven to bake for 30 minutes.
- Once crisp around the edges, take it out of the oven, leave to cool and season with salt and pepper.

Turkey Casserole

Ingredients:

- ½ cup, cooked, enriched noodles
- 4 oz. cooked turkey, bite-size pieces
- ½ cup, green beans, divided
- ¼ cup, canned, sliced mushrooms
- 2 tbsp. skim milk
- 1 oz. red onion, chopped
- 1 tsp. chopped pimento
- ¼ tsp. nutmeg
- ¼ tsp. sea salt

Preparation:

- Preheat the oven to 350 degrees.
- Combine the cooked noodles, turkey, green beans and mushrooms in a bowl.
- Add the onion, pimento, nutmeg and seasoning and pour into a baking dish.

- Using a blender, put in the remainder of the green beans and milk, then mix until smooth.
- Add the green bean mix to casserole and mix well.
- Bake for 22 minutes.

Crab Cakes

Ingredients:

- 3 tbsp. low-fat mayonnaise
- 1 free-range/organic egg
- 1 tbsp. mustard
- Juice 1 lemon
- Fresh parsley, chopped
- 500g white crabmeat
- 4 tbsp. breadcrumbs
- 5 tbsp. extra virgin olive oil

For the sauce:

- 3 shallots, diced
- 3 tbsp. thick double cream
- 1 ½ cups, butter, cubed
- 1 lemon, juiced
- 350ml white wine

Preparation:

- Preheat oven to 375 degrees.
- Mix together the mayonnaise, egg, mustard, lemon juice and parsley. Put crabmeat in and add the breadcrumbs. Chill for 25 minutes then shape into 6 cakes.

- Heat in a frying pan, heat the olive oil and allow the crab cakes to brown on both sides. Bake in the oven for 12 minutes or until cooked through.

For the sauce:

- Boil the white wine, shallots and thyme until reduced.
- Add the cream and bring back to the boil. Then, remove from the heat and slowly add the butter, whisking constantly. Complete the sauce by adding fresh lemon juice and season to taste. Serve together.

Orzo Meatballs

Ingredients:

- Handful, fresh basil, chopped
- 1 pack, minced beef
- 2 garlic cloves, crushed
- 1 tbsp. dried oregano
- 1 tbsp. extra virgin olive oil
- 1 jar, tomato passatta
- 3 cups, orzo
- Parmesan, finely grated

Preparation:

- Mix the basil with the mince, garlic and oregano and roll into 20-24 meatballs.
- Heat the oil then the meatballs in a frying pan over a high heat and brown each side for 5 minutes. Stir in the passatta and bring to the boil for 5 minutes.
- Then, turn down to a simmer and cook for another 10 minutes.
- Cook the orzo following pack instructions.

- Once cooked and drained, scoop and serve. Top with the meatballs, then sprinkle the Parmesan on top and scatter with the reserved basil leaves. Serve immediately.

Prawn Style Curry

Ingredients:

- 1 tbsp. vegetable oil
- 1 red onion, chopped
- 1 tsp. root ginger
- 2 tsp. red curry paste
- 2 chopped tomatoes, canned
- 4 tbsp. coconut milk
- 1 pack, frozen prawns
- Fresh coriander, chopped

Preparation:

- Heat the oil in a saucepan. Then, add in the onion and ginger and cook for a few minutes until soft.
- Stir in curry paste, then cook for 1 min more and pour over the chopped tomatoes and coconut milk. Bring to the boil, then leave to simmer for 5 minutes.
- Put in the prawns, then cook for 10 minutes more. Serve with plain rice.

Cauliflower Cheese

Ingredients:

- 1 large cauliflower, leaves cut and in chunks.
- 500ml semi-skimmed milk
- 4 tbsp. plain flour

- 4 tbsp. unsalted butter
- Handful cheese, grated
- Seasoning

Preparation:

- Preheat the oven to 425 degrees.
- Bring a large saucepan of water to the boil and add the cauliflower, then cook for 5 minutes until soft. Drain the cauliflower and tip into an ovenproof dish.
- Bring the pan back on the heat, then add the milk, flour and butter.
- Whisking it fast as the butter melts and the mixture begins to boil – a sauce will begin to thicken. Whisk for a couple of minutes until the sauce becomes thick.
- Turn off the heat and pour in half of the cheese over the cauliflower. Scatter the remainder of the cheese and breadcrumbs. Serve immediately.

Mexican Pot

Ingredients:

- 2 tbsp. avocado oil
- 1 onion, finely chopped
- 450g pork mince
- 4 chopped tomatoes, canned
- 3 tbsp. tomato puree
- 3 cups, cooked rice
- Fresh parsley, chopped

Preparation:

- Heat oil in a saucepan until hot, then add in the onion and allow it to turn golden, after 5 minutes, stirring occasionally. Add mince to the pan and cook until it's no longer pink.
- Put the tomatoes into the mince and the tomato purée, then give it a good mix and let it come to the boil. Simmer, with the lid covered, for 25 minutes to cook it all through.
- Add in the rice and let the flavours infuse and garnish with parsley.

Kale Chickpea & Bean Stew

Ingredients:

- 1 ½ carrots (chopped)
- 1 ½ sweet bell pepper (chopped)
- 2 handfuls of kale
- 1 clove of garlic (finely sliced)
- 1 butter beans (canned)
- Herbs: thyme, coriander, oregano
- Fresh parsley
- Salt and pepper
- 1 celery stick, chopped
- 1 medium sweet potato, chopped
- 1 red onion chopped, chopped
- 2 chopped tomatoes, canned
- Chickpeas, canned
- 1 glass of water
- Drizzle of extra virgin olive oil

Instructions:

- In baking pot, add the chopped tomatoes and cook it on low to medium heat, stir and add then vegetables. Add one glass of water at the end and let it simmer for 10 minutes on a medium heat.

- Meanwhile, wash the kale and separate the leaves from the stalk. Combine the kale leaves to the pot of tomatoes, then allow to simmer for a further couple minutes.

- Garnish the stew with herbs and let it simmer for a bit longer to allow the herbs infuse together, adding more flavour to the dish.

Creamy Asparagus Pasta

Ingredients:

- 4 ½ cups, fusilli
- 10 asparagus spears (woody ends removed & cut into lengths)
- Large handful, each of frozen peas
- Zest and juice, ½ lemon
- ½ cup, soft cheese

Preparation:

- Cook the pasta by the pack instructions.
- Two minutes nearing the end of the cooking time, add the peas and asparagus.
- Boil everything together for the final extra minutes, then scoop out and reserve a cup of the cooking liquid from the pan before draining.
- Return the pasta and veg into the empty pan and add the lemon zest, soft cheese, seasoning and stir in 3 tbsp. of the cooking liquid to thin the sauce. Serve hot.

Veggie Quinoa Salad with Salmon

Ingredients:

- ¾ cup, quinoa
- 1 tsp. olive oil
- 400ml vegetable stock (bouillon)
- 1 small pack, asparagus (trimmed)
- Small handful, frozen soya beans
- Flaked almonds (toasted)
- 10 fresh broccoli, florets (trimmed &
- Zest and juice 1 lemon
- 2 salmon fillets, 150g each
- ½ garlic clove, crushed
- 20 frozen lentils
- 6 spring onions
- Baby spinach leaves
- Handful mint and parsley, chopped

Preparation:

- Rinse the quinoa and tip into a large frying pan. On a medium, dry out the quinoa, whilst stirring. Once all the liquid has evaporated, add in the oil.
- Cook the quinoa until it has turned brown and starts to pop, this will take 12 minutes to reach. Stir to stop the quinoa from burning. Add the stock and simmer for 18 minutes until all the liquid is incorporated. Pour into a dish and allow to cool.
- Meanwhile, bring a saucepan filled with water to the boil. Place the frozen soya beans, asparagus and broccoli in and simmer for 2 minutes. Remove veg from the pan, using a straining spoon and put it into a bowl of ice-cold water. Then, drain the veg.

- Add a few drops of the lemon juice to the pan with the stock water, then turn the heat down to a gentle simmer.

- Season the salmon fillets and put them into the water fully. Poach for 7 minutes until just about cooked. Remove and allow to cool, then peel off the skin and part into big chunks.

- To make a dressing, mix together the garlic, most of the lemon zest and the left over lemon juice.

- Combine together in a large bowl the quinoa, vegetables, lentils, spring onions, herbs, spinach and dressing, then season. Put onto a serving plate, top with salmon, then scatter over almonds.

Snacks

Aubergine Slider

Ingredients:

- 3 tbsp. extra virgin olive oil
- 2 aubergines, sliced
- 4 tomatoes
- 1 ball, mozzarella, sliced
- Basil leaves

Preparation:

- Preheat the oven to 390 degrees.
- Grease an oven tray.
- Place the aubergine slices on the oven tray and drizzle with oil
- Bake in the oven for 25 minutes until softened.
- Once cooked top each aubergine with mozzarella and a tomato. Place on serving plates. Return to oven for another 5 minutes or until the cheese has melted. Scatter over some basil leaves. Serve hot.

Chocolate Oranges

Ingredients:

- 5 oranges, mandarins or clementine's (peeled and separated)
- ½ cup dark chocolate pieces
- Sea salt

Preparation:

- Line a baking tray with parchment paper.
- Place the chocolate pieces into a small glass bowl and place over boiling water in a saucepan, medium to low heat.

- Once the chocolate has melted, take each orange slice and dip it halfway in the chocolate, place it onto the tray, then place into the fridge to harden the chocolate.
- Place them into a serving bowl and enjoy!

Almond and Coconut Macaroons

Ingredients:

- 2 cups unsweetened desiccated coconut
- ½ cup almond slices
- 2 chia egg whites
- ¼ cup raw honey
- 1 tsp vanilla extract

Preparation:

- Preheat oven to 350F.
- Line your baking tray with baking paper.
- In a mixing bowl, whisk the honey and chia egg whites.
- Then, add the desiccated coconut, vanilla extract and almonds and mix everything together.
- Take a soup spoon and scoop up some of the mixture and form the dough into individual macaroons, place onto the baking tray and into the oven for 12 mins.
- When they turn golden brown, take them out of the oven, let them cool down and then serve.

Sun-dried Tomato Couscous Salad

Ingredients:

- 535ml water
- 1 cup, couscous

- 1 tbsp. olive oil
- 3oz sun-dried tomatoes
- 1oz fresh basil leaves
- Feta, crumbled
- Seasoning
- Lemon, halved and squeezed
- 1 ½ bunches spring onions, chopped
- 4 ½ cloves garlic, crushed

Preparation:

- In a bowl, soak the sun-dried tomatoes with water for half an hour, until absorbed. Drain over a bowl, reserving the water. Then, roughly chop the sun-dried tomatoes into little pieces.
- Put a medium saucepan on a medium heat. Then, add the reserved water and bring to the boil.
- Stir in the couscous.
- Remove the pan from heat, then cover using a lid and leave for a couple of minutes. Then, lightly fluff the couscous with a fork.
- Meanwhile, heat the olive oil in a wok. Adding the chopped sun-dried tomatoes, garlic, spring onions and sauté for five minutes, until the spring onions are soft.
- Combine basil and lemon juice then season, to taste.

Coconut Water Fruit Pops

Ingredients:

- 2 kiwis (halved and sliced)
- 8 strawberries (halved)
- 16 blueberries
- 16 raspberries

- Coconut water
- Popsicle molds

Preparation:

- Fill the popsicle molds with an equal amount of the fruit.
- Then fill with coconut water to the top.
- Place the popsicle sticks on top of each, then place into the freezer and freeze for at least 5 hours or until solid.
- Take them out of the freezer and enjoy!

Ambercup Coconut Milk Treat

Ingredients:

- 1 ambercup squash (Pumpkin substitute)
- 2 cups coconut milk
- ¼ cup raw honey
- 2 tsp ground cinnamon
- 1 chia egg white
- ¼ tsp nutmeg

Preparation:

- Start by cutting the top off of the squash and spoon out all of the seeds inside.
- Place the squash into a large saucepan and add with a few inches of water, but not enough to cover the squash. Place onto a plate and set aside.
- Simmer over a medium heat for about 15 minutes until the flesh inside is soft.
- In a bowl, add the honey, coconut milk, chia egg white, cinnamon and nutmeg and stir to combine.

- Pour the coconut mixture into the squash, use it as a bowl. Eat the squash as with the coconut mixture. Serve and enjoy!

Baked Apple Chips

Ingredients:

- 2 or 3 apples
- Ground cinnamon to taste

Preparation:

- Preheat oven to 220F.
- Line a baking tray with parchment paper and set aside.
- Slice the apples thinly and place onto the baking tray. Dust some cinnamon on top of them and place them into the oven for 1 hour.
- Then flip the slices and cook for another hour.
- Take them out of the oven and allow them to cool.
- Serve and enjoy this tasty little treat!

Creamed Spinach

Ingredients:

- 2 cups baby spinach
- 2 cups coconut milk
- 1 onion (finely chopped)
- 3 crushed garlic cloves
- 2 tbsp. tapioca starch
- Pinch ground nutmeg
- Pinch cayenne pepper

- 3 tbsp. ghee or sunflower seed butter
- Sea salt

Preparation:

- In a saucepan melt the ghee over a medium heat.
- Then slowly whisk in the tapioca starch and cook for 5 minutes.
- Add the garlic and onion to the saucepan and cook for another minute.
- Then add all of the spinach and cook until softened.
- Add in the cayenne pepper, coconut milk and nutmeg, stir everything and cook for another 5 minutes.
- Season with sea salt and serve.

Carrot and Rutabaga Mash

Ingredients:

- 1 ¼ cup rutabaga (peeled and chopped)
- 1 ¼ cup carrots (peeled and chopped)
- 4 tbsp. ghee
- 1 tbsp. fresh parsley
- Sea salt
- Black pepper

Preparation:

- Place the rutabaga and carrots into a large saucepan and cover with water.
- Bring the water to a boil on medium heat and reduce to a simmer. Then cover with a lid slightly and let it simmer for 20 minutes or until really soft.

- Drain water and mash with a masher and add the ghee.
- Season with the salt and pepper and sprinkle with fresh parsley to serve.

Berry Crumble

Ingredients:

- 4 cups fresh or frozen mixed berries
- 1 cup almond meal
- ½ cup ghee or almond butter
- 1 cup oven roasted walnuts, sunflower seeds, pistachios.
- ½ tsp ground cinnamon

Preparation:

- Preheat oven to 350F.
- Crush the nuts using a mortar and pestle.
- In a bowl, combine the nut mix, almond meal, cinnamon and ghee and combine well.
- In a pie dish, spread half the nut mixture over the bottom of the dish, then top with the berries and finish with the rest of the nut mixture.
- Bake for 30 minutes and serve warm with natural vanilla yogurt.

Chocolate Banana Boats

Ingredients:

- 2 bananas
- ½ cup dark chocolate (broken into pieces)
- 2 tbsp. desiccated coconut

Preparation:

- Preheat oven to 300F.
- Do not remove the banana skin, just slice the skin down one side of the banana.
- Fill each banana with the chocolate pieces and desiccated coconut.
- Roll each banana in foil and place on a baking tray.
- Cook for 20 – 25 minutes.
- Serve hot.

Marinated Beets

Ingredients:

- 3 cups sliced beets
- 2 onions (sliced in thin rounds)
- 1 tbsp. ghee
- 2 sprigs fresh thyme
- 1 cup white wine vinegar
- ½ tsp sea salt
- 6 garlic cloves
- Pinch black pepper
- 2, 1 quart jars

Preparation:

- Preheat oven to 400F.
- Prepare the beets by scrubbing them of any excess dirt and remove the root and stems.
- Line a large baking dish with foil and place the beets onto there and drizzle with one tablespoon of ghee.

- Garnish them with thyme. Then seal the excess foil over the beets and roast for 1 to 1 ½ hours until soft.

- Now, remove from the oven and allow to cool. When they are warm remove the skin, then allow to cool completely.

- Place the onions into a large bowl and cover with hot water so that they begin to tender, for 10 minutes.

- When the beets have cooled, slice them into ¼ inch rounds.

- Once the 10 minutes has passed, start layering the onions and beets in the jars.

- In a small mixing bowl, add the salt, cloves, pepper and vinegar, mix to combine. Then, pour half of the mixture into each jar.

- Seal the jars then place them into the fridge for at least one day before serving.

Coffee Flavored Chocolate Mousse

Ingredients:

- ¼ cup dark chocolate chips or squares
- 1 tbsp. ground coffee beans
- 1 tbsp. vanilla extract
- ½ cup coconut milk
- ¼ cup boiling water
- ¼ tsp mint extract

Preparation:

- In a medium skillet, melt the chocolate over a low heat to prevent burning and stir frequently with a wooden spoon.

- Add in the coconut milk and combine with the chocolate.

- In a small bowl, mix the boiling water with the ground coffee beans.

- Now, combine the coffee bean mixture, chocolate mixture, vanilla and mint extract.
- Pour the mixture into 2 large dessert dishes and place into the fridge for 2 - 3 hours. To allow them to become firm.
- Take them out of the fridge and enjoy!

Maple Roasted Parsnip Chips

Ingredients:

- 5 cups parsnips
- ¼ cup coconut oil
- 3 tbsp. maple syrup

Preparation:

- Preheat oven to 392°F.
- Peel the parsnips, cut them into chip sizes and place them into an oven proof dish.
- Drizzle with coconut oil generously until covered and then do the same with the maple syrup.
- Bake in the oven for 15 minutes, until crisp.
- Remove from the oven and turn them over to cook on the other side for another 10 – 15 mins.
- Remove from oven, allow to cool and then serve.

Baked Fruit with Custard

Ingredients:

- 1 large pot of pre-made natural vanilla custard
- 2 sliced green apples
- 2 sliced bananas

- 2 stalks of rhubarb (also sliced)
- 2 tbsp. cinnamon

Preparation:

- Preheat oven to 325°F.
- In a parchment lined oven dish, place the sliced apples and rhubarb and sprinkle with cinnamon and bake for 15 minutes, until tender.
- Take out of the oven, wait for them to cool slightly, then transfer onto a glass oven proof dish, along with the sliced banana and sprinkle with a little more cinnamon and cover with the vanilla custard.
- Bake for another 2 – 5 minutes, until baked slightly.
- Serve warm.

Dessert Recipes

Apple, Strawberry & Macadamia Crumble

Ingredients:

- 3 apples, cut into thin wedges (keep skin)
- 1 tsp. cinnamon
- 1 cup, almond flakes
- ¼ cup, macadamias
- 1 tbsp. chia seeds
- ½ cup, coconut oil
- 2 tsp. vanilla extract
- 14 strawberries, sliced into quarters
- ½ cup, oats
- ¼ cup, pumpkin seeds
- 3 tbsp. maple syrup

Preparation:

Filling:

- Place the strawberries and apples into a steamer basket over a pot of simmering water, sprinkle with cinnamon and place the lid on top.
- Simmer for approximately 5 minutes or until the apples are soft.
- Put the steamed apple and strawberries into a baking dish, spreading the fruit to cover the entire surface of the base of the dish.

Crumble:

- Preheat the oven to 320 degrees.
- In a bowl, mix together all dry ingredients.

- Melt the coconut oil and pour over the dry ingredients. Before mixing it in, add in the liquid sweetener and vanilla extract and stir well.

- The crumble mix should form a ball when squeezed together with your palms. If not, add more coconut oil to the "doughy" mix.

- Spread the crumble mix over the top of the fruit aligned in the baking dish and cover it completely.

- Bake for 15 minutes or until the crumble turns golden. Serve hot.

Panna Cotta with Compote

Ingredients:

For Panna Cotta:

- 3 tsp. gelatin
- 2 tbsp. water
- 500ml soya milk
- 1 lemon, zested
- 2 tbsp. caster sugar

For Compote:

- 8 ripe peaches, stoned and halved
- 150 ml. water
- ¼ cup, caster sugar
- 1 vanilla pod, split and scooped

Preparation:

For Panna Cotta:

- Add the gelatin to water and soak for 5 minutes.

- Meanwhile, in a saucepan add soya milk, zest, vanilla pod, sugar. Heat until the liquid just about comes to the boil, then remove from the heat and stir in the gelatin.

- Cool for 10 minutes. Strain the milk mixture and divide between 4 ramekins. Cover with cling film and refrigerate for 1 ½ hours until set.

For Compote:

- In a saucepan, combine caster sugar and water and heat until the sugar has dissolved.

- Add the peaches and cook over a gentle heat for 15 minutes or until the peaches are soft, then leave to cool. Serve along with the panna cotta.

Pear Tarte Tatin

Ingredients:

- 8 pears, cored, peeled and halved
- ½ cup, caster sugar
- 1/3 cup, unsalted butter
- 500g puff pastry
- 3 cardamom pods
- 1 cinnamon stick
- 2 star anise

Preparation:

- In a saucepan, tip the sugar, butter, star anise, cardamom and cinnamon and place over a high heat, cook until bubbling. Shake the pan and stir the buttery sauce until it separates and the sugar caramelizes.

- Lay the pears in the pan, then cook in the sauce for 10-12 minutes, until completely caramelized. Caramelize as much as you can, they don't burn. Then set the pears aside.
- Heat oven to 390 degrees.
- Meanwhile, roll out the pastry to 2cm in thickness. Now, use a plate a bit larger than the top of the pan to cut out a circle, then make the edges thinner by pressing them down.
- When the pears have cooled slightly, arrange them in the pan.
- Place the cinnamon stick in the pan, with the cardamom pods scattered around it.
- Drape the pastry over the pears, then tuck the edges down the sides of the pan and under the fruit. Prick the pastry, so it doesn't bubble or erupt while in the oven. Bake for 15 minutes.
- Reduce the heat of the oven to 360 degrees and bake for 16 minutes more until the pastry is golden. Leave it to cool in the dish for around 12 minutes until placing it on a pastry plate.

Tiramisu

Ingredients:

- 570ml double cream
- 1 cup, mascarpone
- 75ml Marsala
- 5 tbsp. caster sugar
- 300 ml hot coffee
- 1 pack sponge fingers
- ¼ bar, dark chocolate
- 2 tsp. cocoa powder

Preparation:

- In a bowl combine the Marsala, cream, sugar and mascarpone. Whisk until the mixture holds strong peaks.

- In a glass dish, put the pre-prepared coffee into the dish and coat the sponge fingers until they have soaked the liquid, but isn't too soggy. Layer them on the dish until half has been used, then lather on half of the cream mix. Grate over the chocolate. Then repeat, until everything is used and coat the sponge with cream to top it off.

- Seal and chill in the fridge for an hour before serving.

Gingerbread Roulade

Ingredients:

- 4 tbsp. unsalted butter
- 4 tbsp. golden syrup
- 2 balls, stem ginger
- 4 organic eggs
- ½ tsp. ground cinnamon
- ½ cup, dark muscovado sugar
- 1 cup, plain flour
- ¼ tsp. baking powder
- 2 tsp. ground ginger

For the filling:

- ¾ cup, unsalted butter
- 3 cups, icing sugar
- 3 tbsp. golden syrup

Preparation:

- Heat oven to 375 degrees.
- Grease and line a Swiss roll tin and grease the parchment paper as well.
- In a saucepan, combine golden syrup, butter and ginger and heat until melted and stir regularly, then set aside to cool a little.
- In a mixing bowl, using an electric whisk, blend the eggs and sugar until light, soft peaks form and has doubled in size – this will take about 10 minutes. The mixture is done when it holds a trail from the beaters for about 4 seconds.
- In the same bowl, sift in the flour, baking powder and spices, then pour the melted butter mixture around the sides of the bowl so that it trickles down into the whisked eggs. Very gently fold everything together with a large metal spoon. Next pour it into the Swiss roll tin.
- Bake for 12 mins until just cooked.
- Meanwhile, lay a sheet of baking parchment, big enough to fit the cake and dust with a little sugar. So, when cooked, you can tip the cake directly onto the parchment.
- Using a knife, on the cake score a line about 2cm from one of the ends, make sure you don't cut the whole way through, this will help to achieve a tighter roll. Carefully roll up from one end to the other, rolling the parchment between the layers. Leave to cool on a wired rack to set the shape.

To make the filling:

- Put the specified ingredients into a bowl, while constantly whisking until smooth. Place in a sandwich bag and cut off one end before piping.

- Flatten the sponge again and cover the entire surface with golden syrup. Squeeze a layer of the filling cream on the inside of the roll, then using the paper, tightly roll again. Then, cut both ends off for a nicer finish.

Caramel Apples

Ingredients:

- 4 cubes of caramel
- 2 small chopped apples
- 5 tbsp. of water

Preparation:

- Place the chopped apples onto a greased baking sheet.
- Place caramels and water in a microwave for 2 minutes, stirring once in-between.
- The, allow to cool briefly.
- Put the apples into the caramel mixture and coat well. Then, leave on the baking sheet to set and cool.

Nutty Fruit Salad

Ingredients:

- 1 kiwi fruit, diced and peeled
- 1 cup diced strawberries
- 1 cup raspberries
- 4 tbsp. chopped walnuts
- ½ cup seedless grapes, chopped in half
- 1 tbsp. orange extract
- 2 cups of water

Preparation:

- Prepare the fruit as required.
- Then, add the orange extract and water and place in the fridge for half an hour, before serving.
- Serve with whipped cream.

Strawberry Mousse

Ingredients:

- 3 cups of frozen strawberries
- 2 tbsp. of cane sugar
- ½ cup Neufchatel cheese
- 1 cup of 1% cottage cheese
- 2 packets of unflavored Knox gelatin
- 4 tsp of egg whites mixed with 2 teaspoons of water

Preparation:

- Place the strawberries and sugar in a mixing bowl.
- Mash until smooth.
- In a separate bowl, whisk the cheese, then whisk in the whites.
- Combine both mixtures.
- Then, add in the gelatin and combine well.
- Leave in the fridge to set for an hour.

Cinnamon Rolls

Ingredients:

- 1 cup fat-free milk
- ¼ cup canola oil
- 1/3 cup sugar

- ¼ teaspoon salt
- 2 packages dry yeast
- ¼ cup warm water
- 1 egg
- 2 egg whites
- 3 cups all-purpose (plain) flour
- 2 ½ cups whole-wheat (whole-meal) flour
- 2 tablespoons ground cinnamon
- 3/4 cup brown sugar
- ¼ cup raisins
- ½ cup frozen apple juice concentrate, thawed

Preparation:

- In a small saucepan, heat the milk until just below the boiling point. Don't boil. Stir in the oil, sugar and salt. Remove the milk mixture from the heat and cool until lukewarm.

- In a small bowl, combine yeast and water. Stir and set aside for 5 minutes.

- In a large bowl, beat the egg and egg whites using an electric mixer. Add in the yeast and milk mixture. Using a wooden spoon or a KitchenAid-style countertop mixer, mix in the flours, 1 cup at a time, until a soft dough forms.

- Turn the dough out onto a generously floured work surface and, with floured hands, knead gently until the dough is smooth and elastic, about 5 minutes. If using a countertop mixer, use a dough hook and follow the manufacturer's directions. Return the dough to the bowl and cover with plastic wrap. Let rise in a warm place until double in size, about 1 ½ hours. Divide the dough in half and form into 2 balls. Cover with plastic and let sit for 10 more minutes.

- In a small bowl, combine the cinnamon, brown sugar and raisins.
- Spray an 11-by-14 baking sheet with cooking spray.
- Using a rolling pin, roll each ball of dough into a 16-by-8-inch rectangle. Spray the dough with cooking spray. Sprinkle each rectangle with half of the cinnamon mixture. Starting at the long side, roll up each rectangle. Slice each roll into 16 pieces and place on the prepared baking sheet. Let rise until double in size, about 1 ½ hours.
- Preheat the oven to 350° F.
- In a saucepan, heat the apple juice over medium heat. Cook until the juice is syrupy, about 5 to 7 minutes. Brush each roll with the apple juice. Bake until golden brown, about 15 minutes. Serve warm.

Rhubarb Pecan Muffins

Ingredients:

- 1 cup all-purpose (plain) flour
- 1 cup whole-wheat (whole-meal) flour
- ½ cup sugar
- 1 ½ teaspoons baking powder
- ½ teaspoon baking soda
- ½ teaspoon salt
- 2 egg whites
- 2 tablespoons canola oil
- 2 tablespoons unsweetened applesauce
- 2 teaspoons grated orange peel
- 3/4 cup calcium-fortified orange juice
- 1 ¼ cup finely chopped rhubarb
- 2 tablespoons chopped pecans

Preparation:

- Preheat the oven to 350 F. Line a muffin pan with paper or foil liners.

- In a large mixing bowl, combine the flours, sugar, baking powder, baking soda and salt. Stir to mix evenly.

- In a separate bowl, add the egg whites, canola oil, applesauce, orange peel and orange juice. Using an electric mixer, beat until smooth. Add to the flour mixture and blend just until moistened but still lumpy. Stir in the chopped rhubarb.

- Spoon the batter into 12 muffin cups, filling each cup about 2/3 full. Sprinkle ½ teaspoon of chopped pecans onto each muffin and bake until springy to the touch, about 25 to 30 minutes. Let cool for 5 minutes, then transfer the muffins to a wire rack to cool completely.

Cranberry Delight

Ingredients:

- 1 quart reduced-calorie cranberry juice
- ½ cup fresh lemon juice
- 1 quart carbonated water
- ¼ cup sugar
- 1 cup raspberry sherbet
- 10 lemon or lime wedges

Preparation:

- Refrigerate the cranberry juice, lemon juice and carbonated water until cold.

- In a large pitcher, mix together the cranberry juice, lemon juice, carbonated water, sugar and sherbet. Pour into tall chilled glasses and garnish with a lemon or lime wedge. Serve immediately.

Orange Rhubarb Marmalade on Toast

Ingredients:

- 2 medium oranges
- 3 cups fresh unsweetened sliced rhubarb
- 1 medium lemon
- 1 ½ cups of water
- ⅛ tsp. baking soda
- 5 cups of sugar
- ½ of a 6 ounce package of liquid fruit pectin (1 foil pouch)

Preparation:

- Remove peels from oranges and lemon and scrape off the white pulp that is beneath. Cut peels into very thin strips.
- Combine peels, rhubarb, water and baking soda and bring to a boil. Cover and simmer for 20 minutes. Do not drain.
- Remove membranes from the fruit and break into sections, discarding seeds and saving the juice.
- Add fruits and juices to the peel mixture and return to boiling. Cover and simmer for 10 minutes.
- Measure out 3 cups of this mixture and put it into another pan with the sugar. Again, bring this to a full rolling boil and let it continue to boil for a full minute.
- Remove it from the heat. Skim off any foam and ladle the mixture into sterilized jars leaving ¼ inch headspace. Once lidded, process in boiling water for 15 minutes. Serve on toast.

Cherry Pie

Ingredients:

- 2 cups cherries

- 1 cup, almond flakes
- ¼ cup, macadamias
- 1 tbsp. chia seeds
- ½ cup, coconut oil
- 2 tsp. vanilla extract
- ½ cup, oats
- 3 tbsp. maple syrup

Preparation:

Filling:

- Place the cherries into a steamer basket over a pot of simmering water and place the lid on top.
- Simmer for approximately 5 minutes or until the apples are soft.
- Put the steamed apple and strawberries into a baking dish, spreading the fruit to cover the entire surface of the base of the dish.

Pastry:

- Preheat the oven to 320 degrees.
- In a bowl, mix together all dry ingredients.
- Melt the coconut oil and pour over the dry ingredients. Before mixing it in, add in the liquid sweetener and vanilla extract and stir well.
- The pastry mix should form a ball when squeezed together with your palms. If not, add more coconut oil to the "doughy" mix.
- Spread the mix on the base of the pie dish
- Place the filling over it and bake until golden. Serve hot.

Chocolate Swiss Roll

Ingredients:

- 4 tbsp. unsalted butter
- 4 tbsp. golden syrup
- 1 bar of chocolate, melted
- 4 organic eggs
- ½ tsp. ground cinnamon
- ½ cup, dark muscovado sugar
- 1 cup, plain flour
- ¼ tsp. baking powder

For the filling:

- ¾ cup, unsalted butter
- 3 cups, icing sugar

Preparation:

- Heat oven to 375 degrees.
- Grease and line a Swiss roll tin and grease the parchment paper as well.
- In a saucepan, combine golden syrup, butter and melted chocolate and heat until melted and stir regularly, then set aside to cool a little.
- In a mixing bowl, using an electric whisk, blend the eggs and sugar until light, soft peaks form and has doubled in size – this will take about 10 minutes. The mixture is done when it holds a trail from the beaters for about 4 seconds.
- In the same bowl, sift in the flour, baking powder and spices, then pour the melted butter mixture around the sides of the bowl so that it trickles down into the whisked eggs. Very gently fold

everything together with a large metal spoon. Next pour it into the Swiss roll tin.

- Bake for 12 minutes until just cooked.

- Meanwhile, lay a sheet of baking parchment, big enough to fit the cake and dust with a little sugar. So, when cooked, you can tip the cake directly onto the parchment.

- Using a knife, on the cake score a line about 2cm from one of the ends, make sure you don't cut the whole way through, this will help to achieve a tighter roll. Carefully roll up from one end to the other, rolling the parchment between the layers. Leave to cool on a wired rack to set the shape.

The filling:

- Put the specified ingredients into a bowl, while constantly whisking until smooth. Place in a sandwich bag and cut off one end before piping.

- Flatten the sponge again and cover the entire surface with golden syrup. Squeeze a layer of the filling cream on the inside of the roll, then using the paper, tightly roll again. Then, cut both ends off for a nicer finish.

CHAPTER 6 – 2 WEEK MEAL PLAN

I tend to keep to 5-10 core recipes for each meal, and at times I won't have any dessert or snacks throughout the day. I don't require a lot of variety in my food to keep my diet on track. I enjoy food, but I see it as fuel. I've also been on the Zone Diet for several years and it's taken me some time to know what I like, and what works for me.

I know a lot of people that have struggled with other diet plans they've tried due to the lack of variety in their meals and not knowing how to put it all together in a Meal Plan format.

In the previous chapter I presented a large number of recipes that fit within the Zone Diet, and I've taken it a step further in this chapter by putting it all together in a 2 Week Meal Plan. You are welcome to change some of the recipes around that appeal to you more, but I would encourage you to try the recipe before you judge them.

Week 1:

Day One:

Breakfast: Breakfast Sandwich

Lunch: Vegetable Stuffed Cabbage

Snack: Aubergine Slider

Dinner: Gluten Free Cauliflower Salad

Dessert: Apple, Strawberry & Macadamia Crumble

Day Two:

Breakfast: Fruit Salad

Lunch: Udon Noodle Salad with Almond Dressing

Snack: Chocolate Oranges

Dinner: Roasted Butternut Squash with Broccoli Pesto Filling

Dessert: Panna Cotta with Compote

Day Three:

Breakfast: Apple Cinnamon Crepe

Lunch: Cabbage, Lettuce & Leek Stir Fry

Snack: Almond and Coconut Macaroons

Dinner: Roasted Red Pepper and Pesto Courgette with Savoury Scones

Dessert: Pear Tarte Tartin

Day Four:

Breakfast: Breakfast Quesadilla

Lunch: Jamaican Rice & Peas

Snack: Sundried Tomato & Couscous Salad

Dinner: Pan-Fried Festive Salad

Dessert: Tiramisu

Day Five:

Breakfast: Nut & Berry Smoothie

Lunch: Lentil Dahl

Snack: Coconut Water Fruit Pops

Dinner: Ratatouille

Dessert: Gingerbread Roulade

Day Six:

Breakfast: Steak and Eggs

Lunch: Mushroom & Tofu Stroganoff

Snack: Ambercup Coconut Milk Treat

Dinner: Spinach Quiche

Dessert: Caramel Apples

Day Seven:

Breakfast: Oatie Porridge

Lunch: Quinoa Pasta, Peas and Kale with Vegan Alfredo Sauce

Snack: Baked Apple Chips

Dinner: Turkey Casserole

Dessert: Nutty Fruit Salad

Week 2:

Day One:

Breakfast: Rice Bowl

Lunch: Stuffed Bell Peppers

Snack: Creamed Spinach

Dinner: Crab Cakes

Dessert: Strawberry Mousse

Day Two:

Breakfast: Blueberry Ricotta Oatmeal

Lunch: Tomato & Aubergine Pasta

Snack: Carrot and Rutabaga Mash

Dinner: Orzo Meatballs

Dessert: Cinnamon Rolls

Day Three:

Breakfast: Breakfast Tart

Lunch: Coconut Chana Saag

Snack: Berry Crumble

Dinner: Prawn Style Curry

Dessert: Rhubarb Pecan Muffins

Day Four:

Breakfast: Banana, Almond & Coconut Smoothie

Lunch: Curried Potato

Snack: Chocolate Banana Boats

Dinner: Cauliflower Cheese

Dessert: Cranberry Delight

Day Five:

Breakfast: Blueberry Breakfast Cookie

Lunch: Tortilla Wraps Tex-Mex Style

Snack: Marinated Beets

Dinner: Mexican Pot

Dessert: Orange Rhubarb Marmalade on Toast

Day Six:

Breakfast: Zucchini Fritters

Lunch: Layered Vegetable Bake

Snack: Coffee Flavored Chocolate Mousse

Dinner: Kale Chickpea and Bean Stew

Dessert: Cherry Pie

Day Seven:

Breakfast: Carrot Muffins

Lunch: Curry Tomato Soup with Zucchini Noodles

Snack: Maple Roasted Parsnip Chips

Dinner: Creamy Asparagus Pasta

Dessert: Chocolate Swiss Roll

SUMMARY

The Zone diet has tremendous benefits, such as permanent weight loss consistently of around 1-1.5 pounds per week (until you reach your ideal weight), the prevention of cardiovascular diseases and overall improvement of physical health, a stronger immune system, decreases the signs of aging, improves skin tone and overall physique.

A lot of people underestimate the impact that their diet has on their lives, that is why they stick to old routines and fail at new diets that are the hype in that moment, because as the hype fades so does the weight loss goal. Falling back into old routines, are unfortunately very common but if you understand and follow this diet plan you will be sure to get results, I promise you.

This plan is divided into blocks so there is no need to go through the rigorous process of counting your nutritional intake every time you have a meal. It is already pre-calculated making the process seamless and effortless. The Zone diet is a proven way to help you lose fat and gain muscle mass quickly by the Scientific American Frontiers.

The Zone Diet really works well with the Cross Training exercise in particular (Functional Fitness, CrossFit etc.), as well as simpler forms of fitness training. Anyone who is open-minded and serious about losing weight will have great success with this diet and the best thing is that you don't need to go through a drastic lifestyle change you can easily adjust your lifestyle to this plan and that is why it is a great sustainable form of shedding the fat and replacing it with muscle.

If you aren't interested in Cross Training or exercise in general, I would encourage you to start, but the diet will have a larger impact on your appearance, mentality and health than exercise alone, so you've made a great start by following the Zone Diet.

Good luck on making this your final journey to losing fat, looking after your body and feeling fantastic!

ANOTHER TITLE BY TJ WILLIAMS

Cross Training – The Complete Cross Training Guide 1,000 WOD's for Beginners to Beasts

Made in the USA
San Bernardino, CA
22 May 2016